Behold Thy Mother

BEHOLD
THY
MOTHER

by Shirley Burden

DOUBLEDAY & COMPANY, INC.   GARDEN CITY, NEW YORK, 1965

Also by Shirley Burden
I WONDER WHY...

GOD IS MY LIFE

Then the light turned to darkness
for his hour was at hand.

When Jesus therefore had seen his mother and
the disciple standing whom he loved, he saith
to his mother: Woman, behold thy son.
After that, he saith to the disciple:
Behold thy mother.

8

Mary is everywhere now.

High in the Pyrenees
the River Gave
springs from the earth.

It flows through the green fields of France
past a small village called Lourdes.

Bernadette Soubirous was born there in 1844.

Bernadette SOUBIROUS

As a child she tended sheep in the fields
near the village of Bartres.

Her thoughts may not have been of Mary
one day when she was returning home to Lourdes,

but Mary must have been there
and was pleased with the child she saw.

The following day she spoke to Bernadette
as she was gathering firewood
by the River Gave.

No one has seen Mary there since,

but man has built a cathedral,
stone by stone,
in memory of that meeting,

and there are cures that are unexplainable
if we are to believe the word
of medical authorities.

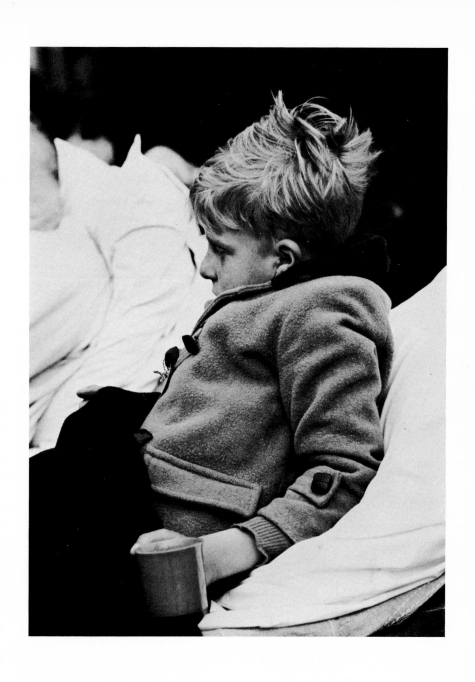

Are they miracles?

Is it faith?

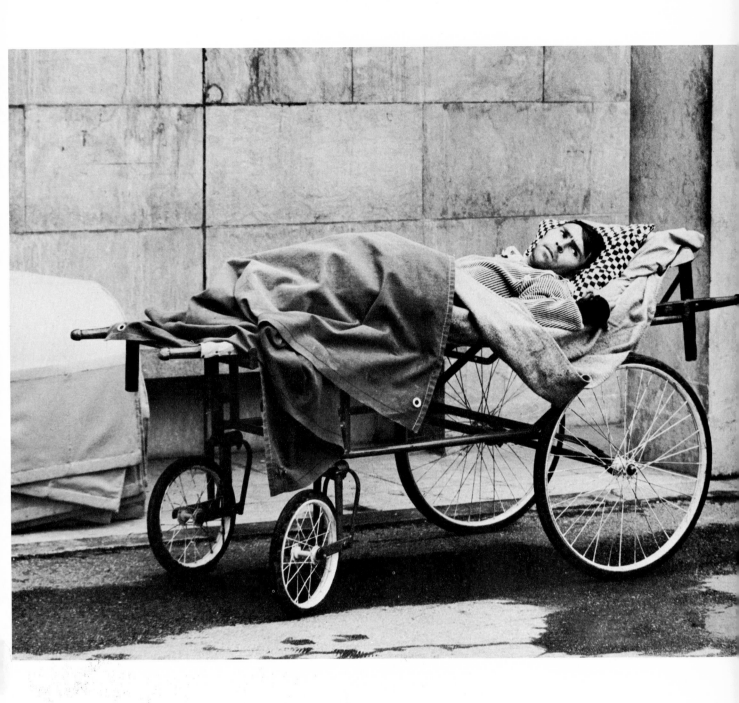

Hope?

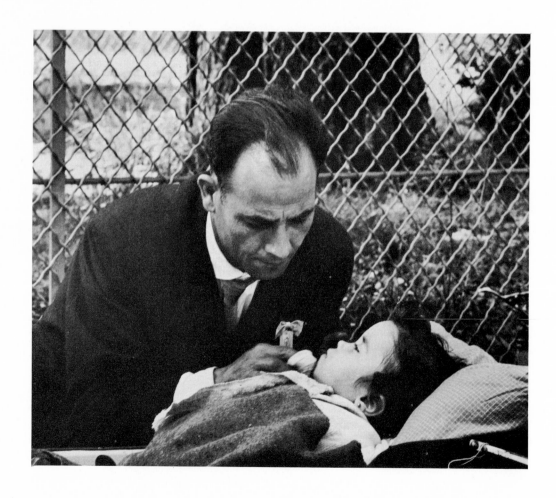

Love?

To some a miracle doesn't exist
because it can't be explained,

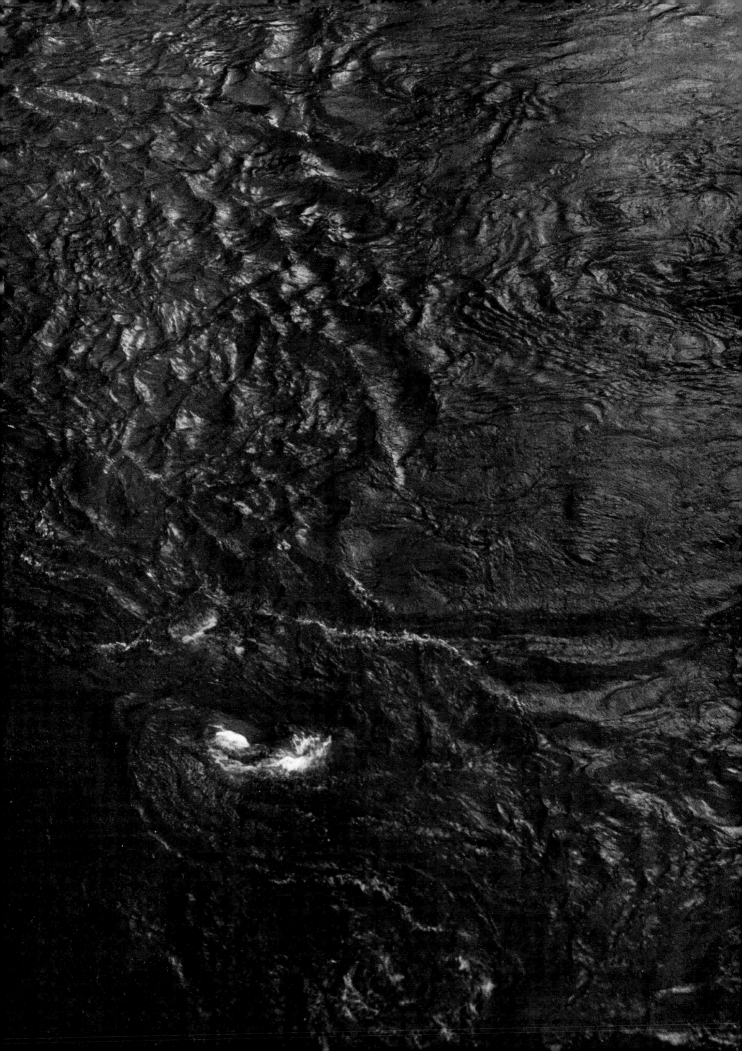

to others
an explanation isn't necessary.

It has ever been thus.
Christ performed many miracles.

Some believed without proof,

others believed not,
because they feared what they could not understand.

Many kinds of people
come to Lourdes each year.

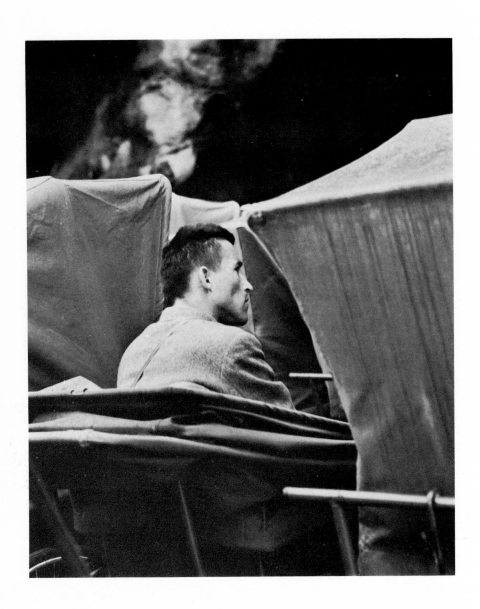

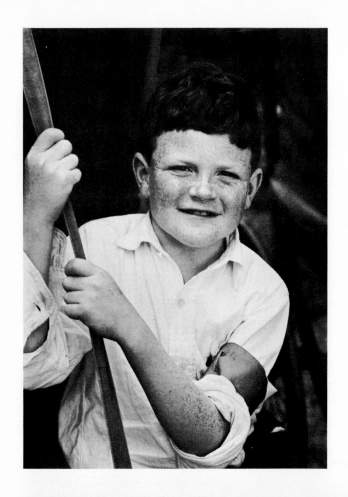

The Mary they find may be made of plaster,

and comes in all shapes, sizes, and prices.

Her meeting with Bernadette,
her rosary,

even her Son

are by the gross.

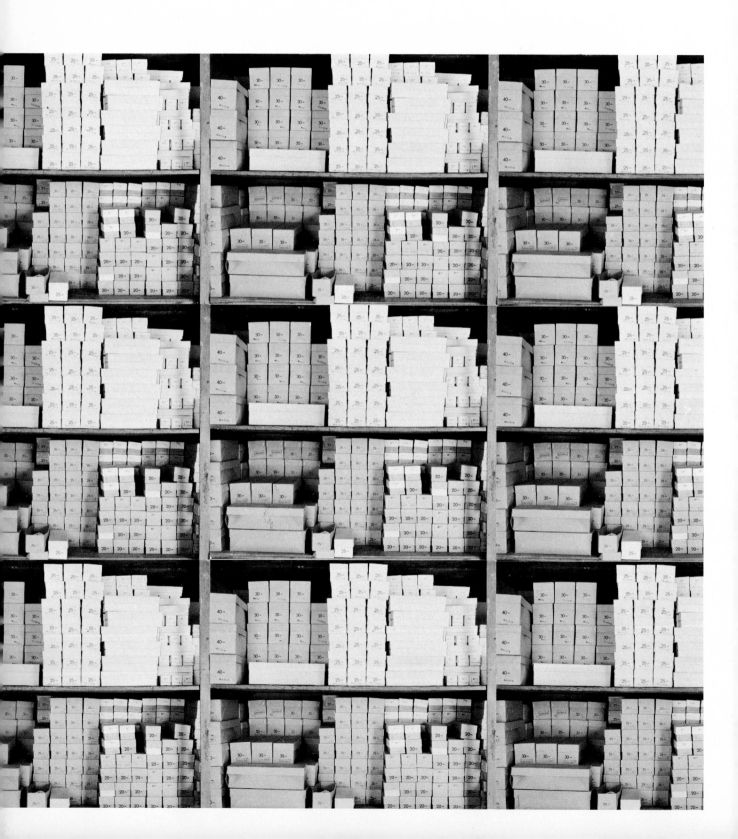

Perhaps they find Mary

at the side of a stretcher bearer

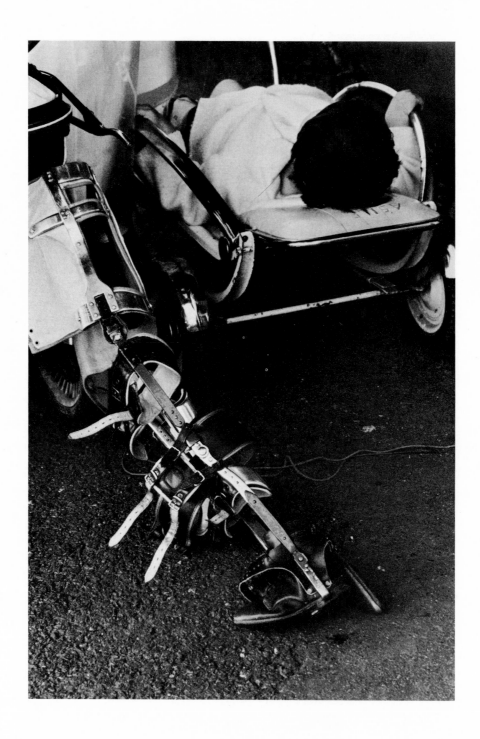

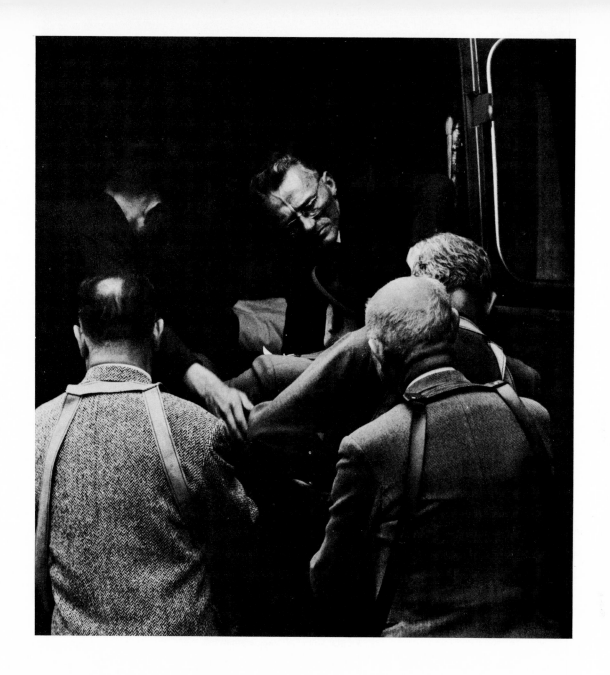

who loves his neighbor enough
to come year after year to help him.

Or they see her
in the heart of a nun

who lives to comfort others.

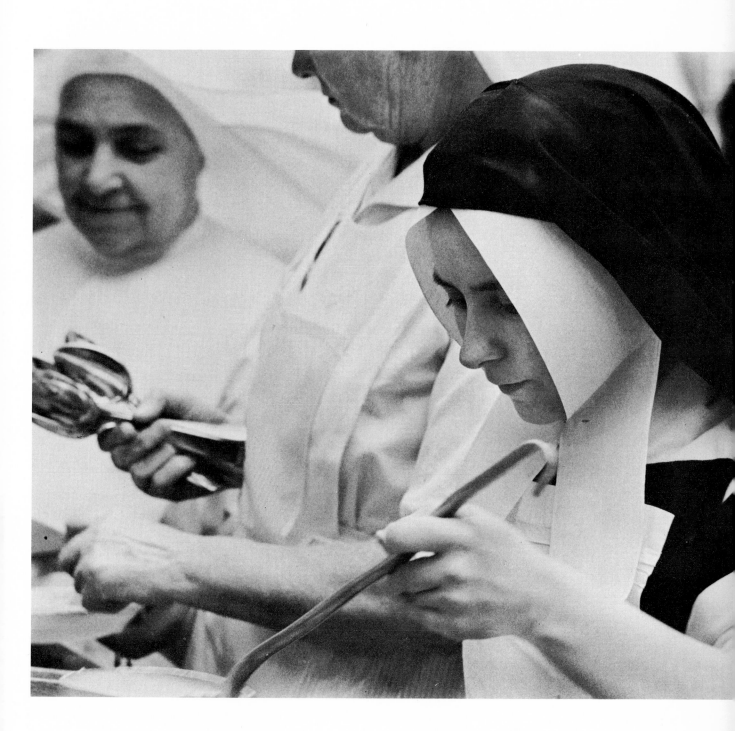

Will Mary come to them,
as she did to Bernadette?

Will she speak to them?

Will she tell her Son of their prayers?

She seems so near,
so very near.

Their voices
fill the dusk,

"Blessed art thou among women..."

and they will hear again the words "Thy faith hath made thee whole."

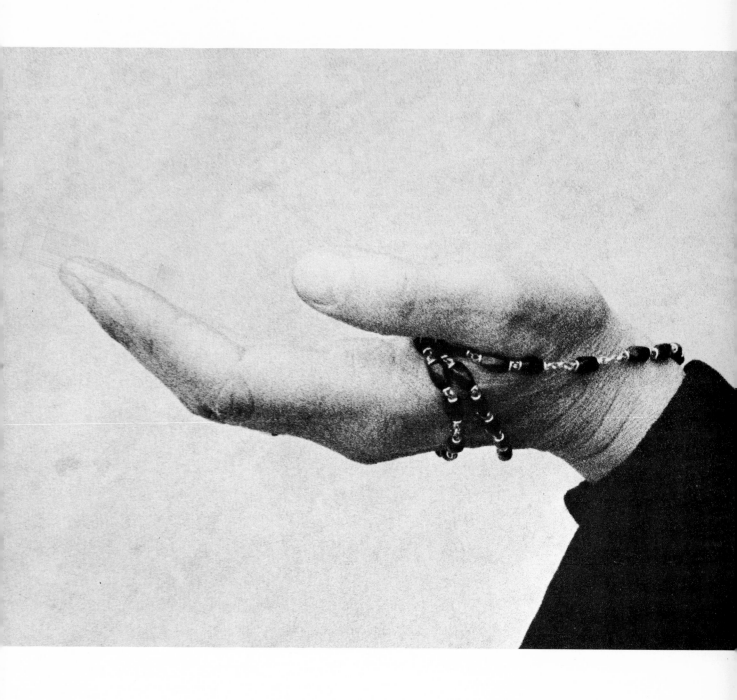